Mimosas at Sunset

Mimosas at Sunset

SHARON M. CARTER

MoonPath Press

Poetry
ISBN 978-1-970256-02-4

Cover art by Sharon M. Carter

Author photo by Paul Hosea

Book design by Tonya Namura using
Mr Eaves (display) and Minion Pro (text)

MoonPath Press, an imprint of Concrete Wolf Poetry Series,
is dedicated to publishing the finest poets
living in the U.S. Pacific Northwest.

MoonPath Press
c/o Concrete Wolf
PO Box 2220
Newport, OR 97365-0163

MoonPathPress@gmail.com

https://MoonPathPress.com

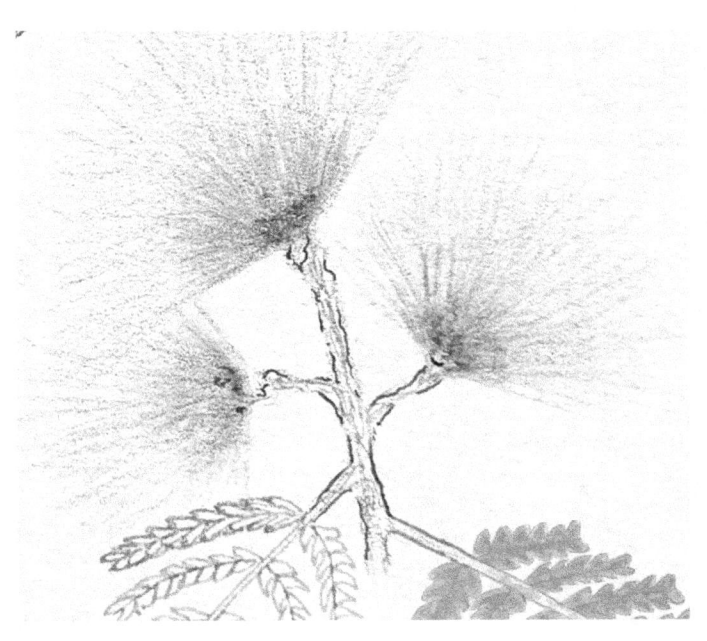

for my flowers, Nicola and Catherine,
and
Mr. Paul

The speech of flowers and other voiceless things.
—Baudelaire

Contents

Mimosas at Sunset

Perennial Climbing Hydrangea

Its flowers grow from spheroid
buds, bald as eggs or moons.
In a strange maturing,
the plant's vines ribbon
around a central stem,
and like a children's story
where the magic egg appears
cracked and spoiled
until a fairy waves her wand,
the hydrangea's homely
shoots unfurl over weeks
into creamy flat-topped blossoms—
intricate florets best described
as flying saucers, leaving
us astonished by such
unexpected beauty.

Honesty

The plant's purple blooms reappear
    every other year,
wave   self consciously
    knowing
they're an invasive species.

Named honesty in one country
    money or moonwort
       elsewhere, their
translucent pods reveal all,
    rattle   silver moons
    or dollars,   each seed
a down payment for the future.

Tell me, when has money
    made anyone honest?
 Our world is dying
       because of it—
decimal points
     have no substance.

On Losing a Douglas Fir

Rot began in the roots
the arborist declares,
crept up xylem and phloem,
to suffocate the entire tree.
His men find a squirrel nest's
galaxy of leaves halfway up;
a punctured birthday balloon;
evidence woodpeckers had drilled
through the firmament
searching for life.

A buzz of chainsaws fills the air
scattering sawdust clouds—
I wince, recall Frost's poem,
the latest hillside cleared for homes.
The tree trunk is lowered
in columns, like dismantling
the Parthenon.
Earth's ruins at my feet.

Blue Torch Cactus

You were the camera's darling,
favoring a three-quarter's view.
This cactus reminds me of you—

its bridal veil flowers trimmed
with fine hair. Your eyes echoed
by its skin's deep blue. You gathered

a like-minded crowd wherever
you roamed, lip-sticked cigarette
held askew, conversation strewn

with *bon mots*. I hear your voice
from memory's vault: Speak up!
Stand straight! Sometimes faint applause.

The hottest part of a flame burns blue—
that detail most reminds me of you.

Mimosas at Sunset

Many gardeners prefer
a cocktail despite the tree's beauty—
blossoms flutter in sunset shades
like flocks of tropical birds.

They argue the long-fingered
seed pods disseminate
too efficiently, creating
monotonous mimosa avenues
especially in warmer lands.

Immense, invasive trees,
short lifespans—
one expert's opinion
on pruning: *any time
you can find a chain saw.*

I say, consider this:
love the beauty
in your life
before it's gone.

Displaced Dogwood

Trucked long distance,
the newest arrive
at the clearing depot,
uprooted
from their previous lives.
Even the driver does not speak
viewing the bedraggled clumps.
Tattered leaves shield
heads from dust and cold.
Without water they stoop
in the thin light, fold
into themselves
as if praying.
After high winds and strife
many gaze back, check
if storm's misery
pursues them.
How they once trusted
the sun, eager faces
embracing the day.

Smoke Trees, Urbino

Green and purple plumes sway
at the verge. Black seed pods scab
their spent flowers. Heat fumes

off asphalt, sun low in the sky—
a red Alfa Romeo swerves
toward someone's dream.

At the villa, history's shadows
stretch across sandstone parapets.
Wind riffles a white tablecloth laid

with silver-rimmed plates, truffle
cheese, flutes of Prosecco.
Business men celebrate—gold

watches, cigars. Smoke trees wave,
their veiled penumbrae warn
of what may lurk hidden.

Blackberries

Little Fistfuls of Blood
        —Sylvia Plath

The image perfects itself, Sylvia might say:
the berries in our collection buckets—
my mother's condition—the four pints of blood
my daughter lost in childbirth and the communion
liquor draining from the sac of boiled fruit.
No end to red.

No end to fistfuls or thorns.
The baby survived, rescued from his own
umbilical garotte, his extraction making
small plucking noises, hands clenching
fistfuls of air.

Worry falling around us like overripe fruit.

Ocean Spray

If we could plant / the ocean inland along / the Pacific
coast / we could touch it / from our decks and /
picnic tables each morning / over coffee / brush
its tumbling / frothy plumes / without getting
wet / buds spiral along / its branches like / water
spurting / from pyramids of leaves / later
summer's creamy flowers / wilt to tan / seeds
like sand caught / in waves' crests / the ocean
erodes the coast / the ocean / takes root inland /

Use Your Alphabet

after Susan Landgraf

Begin with apple blossoms, first pink
then white. Cuttings grafted onto rootstock
fed by xylem and phloem create variants:

Kanzi, Honey Crisp, Querina, Zestar—
names which bolster our expectations.
So much joy in consuming them

we forget we titled their genus
Malus, Greek for evil, forever
burdening them with this symbolism.

Foxgloves

Sometimes I appear pure
white, a Venetian doge's
cap, pretending
to be saintly
and true,
a miracle
cure
for failing
hearts.
More often I dress
in purple,
ripe
and luscious,
my wanton
mouth
open to all.
Risk
the furious
apian within!

Red-Hot Poker

for N.C.S.

I hope you are not offended.
It's the fiery you I see, the dramatic
red spear, shooting off the stalk.
Once a tiny rocket
your trajectory burns through life
leaving a trail of sparks,
gunpowder, stars.
Even your lower florets
opening yellow with pollen
and pistils remind me
of your baby-blond hair.
If wit could be written in numbers
your signifier would be divisible
only by itself.
You might claim sentimentality
has no place in a poem,
but this poem is about recharging
love, the passage of time,
how they intertwine.

Wisteria

We are drawn to you
dressed in your best lilac finery,
growing taller than other varieties.
You spark joy!—intoxicating
displays tempt us into planting.
Why does everything else
about you spell trouble?

We fail to recognize the danger,
import you willingly
for your looks.
Snaking seed pods ensure
your future, stronger
vines undermine native species
as you curve around doorposts
and tree trunks slowly
forcing them
under your control.

Bluebells

Should I pick a bouquet
of melancholy for my table?

Let them hang their lovely
heads in shade—shrouding
the woods in blue, blue, blue.

Herb Robert

a.k.a Stinking Bob

Perhaps emboldened, certainly
unbowed by a distasteful moniker,
you have forced me into servitude.
My gravel paths, mulch, woodlands
strewn with your tarantula stems.
Pretty pink flowers trick the eye,
crane-bill-shaped pods fling seeds
further than my hand-powered spreader.
Every effort to weed unrewarded—
that nasty smell
imparted to my fingers.
New plants emerge overnight.
Bob squats on my land
like a perpetual houseguest.

After a summer of stress
and frustration by fall your leaves
have turned ruby red,
carpet my lawn like the Grand
Staircase at Versailles,
ending the season in splendor.

White Bleeding Heart

So used to our association with blood
your hearts seem waxy.
Early flowers resemble
small purses
from which some might say
a phallus hangs
prior to its reveal into male
and female reproductive parts.
Two sepals peel away
like an old-fashioned Dutch hat,
interior flesh pricked red,
your name a catalog of virtues,
already bled dry.

The Mushroom Chanterelle

Named after the Greek
for *cup* not the French word
to *sing*, their central dimple
neither goblet nor mouth.

At first they languish
in shade, a timid schoolchild
who doesn't fit in. Tumbles
of saffron and muted peach,

their blank faces remain silent
in the forest's symphony.
Once mature their beauty
attracts every forager's knife.

Sautéed in hot buttered pans,
their delicate flavor later described
by diners as: *a hint of apricot
sprinkled with black pepper.*

False Solomon's Seal

This flower is identified as a copycat.
Not just one—it's also known as false
lily of the valley, and false spikenard.

Both Solomons' leaf ladders resemble
each other, surely the prompt
for lazy naming—yet the deceptive

flower's plume, despite its luscious
scent, bears no relation to the namesake's
delicate bells. Humans love to compare!

We extol our arbitrary schemes
for beauty, causing many to favor plastic
faces—a false response to a false premise.

Pity us—that we can appreciate both true
Solomon's seal and its look-alike,
yet needlessly torment ourselves.

Nootka Rose

Your pink-and-green garlands
decorate the Pacific shorelines
of my adopted state—
my yard too, threaded
with persistent roots.
Flowers drape across my septic
system, brief distraction
from potential disruption,
your thorn's misery.

Suckers reappear stronger
every year, thickets
through which Sleeping Beauty's
prince might never slash.
At season's end fat rose hips
interrupt your briars, loved by deer.
My sense of guilt can be profound
after I've grabbed my shears
and cut you down.

Red Satin

Flaming Pieris

White blossoms, inverted
champagne flutes frothy
with pollen, light-filled
among the fiery leaves—
my mother in her ballroom days—
drop crystal earrings, red satin.
Impatient blonde hair.

Saturday afternoons, wet
locks pulled aside, toothbrush
and peroxide ready.
A strange pairing—
the perm's eggy whiff
with her favorite perfume,
"Caliente."

Dressed to dance.
Her blotted lips,
crimson flowers.

Crimson Star Columbine

The flower's petals compare to a cardinal's
red shock against snow, your bridal rose
bouquet, tulip blooms on white linen.

Some associate the flower with blood
from *eagle's talons*, its Latin name, or claim
its hue resembles Jupiter's stormy red spot.

I'd vote for a crimson hot-air balloon
drifting over the Alps at Grenoble, a spin
down Route 101 in my little red Corvette.

Pitcher Plants, Valencia

At the botanical gardens,
visitors ooh and aah
over the pitcher plant's
perverse nature—
ranging from green to red,
full color or striped,
resembling worn condoms—
nectar designed
to attract, lead prey
stumbling over their slippery rims.

Any temptation to insert
a finger
into the sheath
deterred by wall spikes
preventing an easy
withdrawal,
and the pool
of dissolved
insects
at its tip.

Forget-Me-Nots

"Regret nothing," the poem says—
not the unfortunate rendezvous
or those chocolate donuts
floating like galaxies
in their bargain bag.

The child-professor asks
if our mistakes
are like forget-me-nots
which scatter their seeds
and multiply?

Remember, in *The Garden
of Earthly Delights*, strawberry
and thistle flourish side by side.
Humans with bird heads
give birth to snakes.

Childhood Lilac

Their purple grazed
my childhood window—
heady perfume, respite
from cigarette smoke,
burning coal.

They heralded summer's promise,
weeks on local beaches.
Roller skates. Diving boards
at the outdoor swimming pool—
decades long gone.
The house demolished
for a concrete-and-steel
police station where numerous
suspects were roughed up.
Childhood's lost innocence
dancing at memory's edge.
The way blossoms spoil—
brown-tinged,
sweet smell of decay.

Red Rose Bud

for C.L.S.

You are a sublime gift—
full of potential,
classic strength and beauty.
Your petals' secrets fold
toward an interior world.

Attached to a sturdy stem,
your leaves remain fresh,
present honest displays.
Few thorns exist
concealed from view.

Your final destination
remains unknown—
rather than a buttonhole,
Valentine's Day or vase, best
left on stock
displayed as yourself,
hips hinting
at future generations.

You Say Fuchsia...

Memories of once-loved
party dresses;
synthetic pink lipstick,
high heels.

The plant's purple-red flowers
resemble my great-aunt's
earrings—rubies dangle
with glimpses
of her widowed heart.

Relaxing in my porch rocker
I see the flowers turn
like Sufi dancers
on their slender stalks—
a hanging basket,
my meditation.

Violas

to the Window Box Owner

Though it snowed this morning
your pansies waved yellow
hellos as I strolled by
wool-wrapped from frost.
Perhaps you know their name,
derived from the French *pensées,*
meaning thoughts.
An association at odds
with their fancy finger-painted hues,
dreamy hot-day style: Cool Wave
Blueberry Swirl, Jolly Joker,
Matrix Solar Flare.

Some varieties mimic
a scrunched-up Pekinese face
or Yorkie, deep brown
with blushing trim.
Not yours.
Today's window box filled
with purple hearts—
lucky flowers open to the sun,
unaware of the human world
and its judgments.

Notes

Page 7 references an opinion by Steve Bender on pruning mimosas. (SouthernLiving.com)

Page 25: The quotation, "Regret nothing," is from "Antilamentation," by Dorianne Laux.

Acknowledgments

Gratitude to the editors of the following journals for publishing these poems.

"Blackberries," *Ekphrastic Pastiche*
"Bluebells," *Humana Obscura Anthology*
"Blue Torch Cactus," *Wild Roof Journal*
"The Mushroom Chanterelle," *Black Moon Magazine*
"Nootka Rose," *Poets for Science*
"Violas," *Ars Poetica 2025*

Gratitude to Pamela Moore Dionne, Kris Becker, and the late Jayne Marek for midwifing early drafts of several poems. Thanks also to Sheila Bender, Cheryl Merill, and Mara Lathrop for their useful input. Debra Wöhrmann deserves accolades for initiating Thursday's *Poetry Play*, a fun prompt-writing hour, and graciously reading through an early draft of the manuscript.

Mr. Paul's ears have tolerated bad grammar and clichés with aplomb. Thank you once again. Gratitude to Ginny Banks, photographer, whose flower plates ("botanicals") triggered some of my early poems and enhanced the scope of the book.

This book would still be a manuscript in my bedside drawer without Lana Hechtman Ayers, editor of MoonPath Press. Her talents extend from publisher to author of several fabulous poetry collections. Thank you so much!

About the Author

Sharon M. Carter was born in London following its devastation from WW2's Blitz. Her family left to find work in the north of England, settling in a Lancashire seaside resort. Part-time work was freely available, and her early jobs included ice cream seller, waitress, and postwoman. During these decades education was free and this proved pivotal in allowing her to graduate from Cambridge University with a medical degree. Originally trained as a family physician, she was a practicing psychiatrist for over thirty years.

Sharon has lived in London (again), several locations around the UK, a short stint in Greece, and aboard ship as a staff member of the Semester at Sea. She once traveled overland to Nepal. After immigrating in the 1970s via Indiana, she moved to the Pacific Northwest to which she is more firmly attached than a limpet. A lifelong artist working in multiple media she currently devotes most of her time to writing, though there's a subtle interaction.

Sharon is also the author of the poetry book, *Quiver* (Tebot Bach 2022). *Ekphrastic Pastiche*, a book combining poetry and original drawings, was released in 2024. She will always be indebted to the Hedgebrook Foundation for its generosity early in her writing career. The Jack Straw Writers program also provided guidance on presentation. She has co-edited an online literary magazine and helped run a reading series. Other roles have included, cyclist, mother, skier, adventure traveler, and backpacker.

Visit Sharon online at SharonMCarter.com

www.ingramcontent.com/pod-product-compliance
Lightning Source LLC
Chambersburg PA
CBHW071546120626
46550CB00006B/2597

* 9 7 8 1 9 7 0 2 5 6 0 2 4 *